to mySelf be true

to mySelf be true

A simple book to empower women

Reena de la Vega

with Deanna Oyer

Bridges Publishing
Richardson, Texas

Bridges Publishing
2183 Buckingham Rd., Suite 152, Richardson, TX 75081

Cover photograph by Scott Williams of Visual Impressions Photography
Edited by Jacqueline J. Lambiase, Ph.D.
Paintings photographed by Steve Beasley

Library of Congress Catalog Card Number: 98-86000

ISBN: 0-9663675-8-8

First Edition, October 1998

Printed in the United States of America.

This book is dedicated to my parents.

Acknowledgments

Profuse thanks

— to Benny, whose love and practicality have been my best
earthly teachers.

— to my family for their support and their constant faith in me.

— to Elexis Rice for her inspirational, pragmatic and
no-nonsense approach to spirituality.

— to Charlie Baretto for teaching me how to get out
of my head and into my heart, by showing me how
to tap my feeling level effectively.

— to Cristine and George Girgis, who have shown me kindness
and gentleness in its purest human form.

— to Deanna Oyer, an angel of a friend, whose faith
and passion transformed this project into the beautiful
book you now hold in your hand.

I would also like to express my appreciation to Debi Seiler
for the cover design, graphic designs, as well as her valuable
input in making the copy a work of art. Thank you to Defae
Weaver for her unending support with the layout design.
Thanks to everyone at McKool Graphics for their dedication to
high standards in pre-press work and to Great Impressions
for their guidance with production.

TABLE OF CONTENTS

to mySelf be true

Preface

(How to use this book)

Get comfortable with it or take it with you. Read it all the way through or pick out the topics that interest you.

Please use the pages in this book and the Love notes to mySelf sections

to play.

to reflect.

to separate the relevant from the irrelevant.

to make your dreams official and thus real.

to share your fears as you would with a friend
that promises to listen and to help.

If you wish, release your negative feelings by writing them down where you have enough space to let them go. The natural good feelings, which were buried, will resurface.

Like a miner, we pan for that gold. That "gold" has a name.

It is your name.

to mySelf be true

FOREWORD

The premise of this book is that God is my Anchor.

All the tiring and efforted sojourns along the myriad and labyrinthine ways of one's mind or ego are silenced when reminded of this premise.

Everything in our world is a tool to be used to bring us closer to the Light. Then we are in constant communion with God and all doubts about our self-worth are banished. We <u>know</u> we are women of worth and our natural Power shines through.

This is just one woman's way of sharing, perhaps a little raw and awkward at times. In doing so, it is my sincere desire that through the realizations you find in the following pages, you too, will find your peace, center and balance increasingly more each day.

After all ... that is our natural state.

to mySelf be true

I.
TAKING STOCK

Solo I

This pastel painting was done when I agreed to bigger changes and the actions resulting from that decision. During this period, all of my works demonstrated a lot of powerful movements, yet I realized they didn't have to be hectic or harried. To me, power, movement, and their accompanying energy meant a very loving gracefulness.

to mySelf be true

1

ON MEN AND ROMANCE

The great romance never brings the great love. It is the great love that brings the great romance.

I always thought I needed a man to complete me. It was only when I thought of myself as whole and complete that my relationships worked.

Love notes to mySelf

2
ON BEING ALONE

In a constant game of self-deception, we have reluctantly learned that being alone with ourselves is the first step to real happiness. There were many times when it seemed my cries for help went unheeded. I had to reach for that deep, buried and immense hurt before I could resurface. That's when the healing starts.

Love notes to mySelf

3
ON IMPRESSIONS

As women, we are so programmed to be "the perfect little girl," "the perfect 10," whether as wife, mother, girlfriend, lover or friend. In cooperating with these societal dictates for approval, we claw our way to the top of the heap and at each other.

That need not be.

When I started to truly nurture myself, the guilt and sabotaging stopped.

Love notes to mySelf

4
ON PATTERNS

What is this unconscious armoring we do in competing with men? Again and again, it goes back to the need for a healthy self-worth. Having that, there's absolutely no need to compete.

In most instances, authentically valuing ourselves results in a paradoxical loving and nonchalant attitude, and consequently, non-challenging actions.

I have learned that being balanced and centered is the most important thing. It speaks volumes before I even open my mouth.

Love notes to mySelf

5

ON HURT AND REJECTION

I heard that telling about how something or someone in your past has hurt you to everyone and anyone who will listen, even if only in bits and pieces, just energizes and keeps it alive.

But there were times when I hurt so much, I threw all caution to the wind. I scattered my Force and talked too much. Doing this, of course, just guaranteed that I stayed stuck, even though I felt a little relieved temporarily.

The deep dark chasms I found myself in would make me cower in so much fear, that I would instinctively go back to my primal fetal position, when I was safe in God's Womb of Protection.

Only then could I look around me and see that whatever my age, whatever my circumstances … I was always surrounded by an amniotic supportive Force.

It was from this point that I really grew.

Love notes to mySelf

6
ON LEARNING
TO TAKE OUR EMOTIONAL TEMPERATURE

Amid busy days, I forget about God and try to do it all myself instead of going with the Flow. I can always trace the telltale signs toward evening.

Sometimes, getting emotionally sick takes a couple of days while I'm still insisting I'm okay. Consequently, I get tired, depressed—or worse—physically ill.

The warning signs that tell me I am a house divided are:

> losing my keys or locking myself out of my car;

> being overcharged at the store;

> actually being stepped on by a child in the supermarket line;

> being late for appointments in spite of all efforts to make it on time.

The real key, of course, is to stop what you're doing. Pause and catch it early. Notice these clues. It's almost like a nightly examination of conscience!

I need to remember that my life is like the ocean ... there <u>must</u> be an ebb and a flow. One without the other is unnatural.

Like Mother Nature, we must take and make the time to replenish ourselves. To <u>know</u> this is to give yourself only 5 percent of this natural, very loving Energy. To <u>do</u> this, however, is gifting yourself the remaining 95 percent.

Love notes to mySelf

7
ON THOUGHTS
WHILE BUYING LINGERIE

He wanted me to buy the kind of negligee to please him, to please his eye. I bought it only because it delighted me. Giving myself that control satisfied me.

Automatically, and not surprisingly, this feeling of being honest with myself radiates from me whenever I wear the lingerie I like. He just thinks he likes it too, not to mention the great fun we have as a result.

Love notes to mySelf

8
ON BEING KIND TO ONESELF

We always think being kind to ourselves is a compartmentalized part of our life like an occasional bubble bath or a new pair of shoes. It's not. In learning when to say "yes" or "no" to our demanding little world, we learn to be kind to ourselves every single moment. Thus, we release the constant wear and tear on ourselves.

Being kind to ourselves makes it easier to live in the <u>now</u>. It means trusting not some distant God "thing" but a here-and-now God experience.

Being kind to myself means to stop worrying and to just know that all things, not just some, will work out for the best.

One very simple example ... whenever I feel anxious, I purposely make my steps slower. My world will not collapse because of that.

Love notes to mySelf

9

ON INTIMACY

What makes any kind of intimacy energizing is not the energy from the other person. Instead, intimacy energizes when he reacts unconsciously in a positive, loving way because I am comfortable with my own self, my world, and my feelings. He doesn't suspect it but he also wants to tap into that higher and happier vibration. It has everything to do with me ("I am Cause here," I silently say). He just reacts to my energy. The ultimate form of healthy self-love is in surrendering to my own deepest feelings, even beyond surrendering to the man.

Intimacy, translated "into-me-see," is not just a play on words. It is a call for honesty and integrity at its truest and highest level.

I admire women who are serious about their personal growth and spiritual unfolding. These pursuits stop the tidal waves of romantic illusions. As a result, the subconcious high expectations of the other person are removed. After all, most of us grew up in dysfunctional families amid the ongoing cultural and commercial sell of the Prince Charming myth. Thus, we have all these expectations. When we place our faith in the illusion that fairy tales are somehow meant to work, we use our energies unwisely.

We lavish most or all of our hopes on this one person and we get disillusioned because he's human. We worry and age from our unreal expectations.

Acknowledging all this, not just in my head, but making sure I felt and understood it, made it easy to be comfortable with myself. Opening my heart was natural after that. I also forgave myself once again for all the layers of defensiveness I had built up because I was really so afraid. This constant blessing of forgiveness given to myself during my crazy thinking, helped me to not be as afraid, if at all, of any kind of intimacy.

Love notes to mySelf

10

ON USING "MAPS"

Daily journaling is like looking at a map. It shows me where I detoured needlessly and how to avoid it in the future. As a necessary tool and ritual, it makes me face myself squarely instead of playing mind games with the rambling thoughts that can become riotous in my head.

It is like dipping into a fountain of youth and energy. I get my frustrations out of my system, onto paper and I clearly see where I was coming from.

At one time, short of literally kicking someone in the behind and gloating over it, I drew stick figures of the scenarios. Strangely, this had a very healing effect on me. This little technique helped me get in touch with my feelings. I affectionately call this technique "kick 'em stick figures" even though they can represent any scenario. Drawing "kick 'em stick figures" stops me from verbally or non-verbally attacking that person and I am able to say what I really want to say in a kinder, more loving manner.

I go to bed earlier so I can get up earlier to do my journaling, reading and meditating. Done regularly, the process gets faster and outer results in my world get better.

Only after I journal do I go to my to-do list for that day. More likely than not, everything gets done effortlessly and in perfect timing. In retrospect, I see that those items that weren't done were not meant to be done at that particular time.

Keeping a daily journal, like healthy eating, stops
me from cluttering my body. It also helps eliminate one
less worry line from my face.

Love notes to mySelf

to mySelf be true

II.

Setting Forth

Solo II
This work was done with even more love and happiness.
I knew what path to take, knew it was the right way but somehow
still doubted. Like the dancer, I realized I couldn't stay in that
position for too long, lovely though it was. This was when
I started to seriously listen to my inner feelings and against all
my rational thinking—wrote this book.

11

ON ANGER

Being angry is like driving on a long trip with your brakes on. Participating in healthy activities like church, classes, support groups, even volunteer opportunities—all these are almost useless when we are driving with our brakes on. Something will give sooner or later. Quiet, inner rage expressed through the body causes it to be "dis-eased."

I used to wonder why I wasn't reaching all my goals. "What is taking me so long," I asked, "in spite of all these activities related to my personal inner growth?"

Once upon a time, I had cancer. It was a shock, to say the least. I was like that car driving with its brakes on, even though I had been on the path of getting to know God for a considerable time. Luckily I was sane enough to know that sickness was not my natural God-given state. I wanted to prove to myself that all the books I had read about God and how to find Him were <u>true</u>. I also knew my conditional forgiveness was a major block to my complete healing.

In spite of all the medical evidence written in black and white, I knew that God could heal me through the medical process or by other means. I still went through the mainstream medical process even though I wanted to see just what this Power could do through me, if I let It. In short, I didn't buy into the human prognosis even though I was scared.

I always admired the Bible story of Abraham's test of faith and willingness when he was asked to sacrifice his only son. Similarly, the ultimate test of my letting go and letting God was when I stopped hanging on to things in my world. "My kids need me, I still have so much to do, it's not fair and I'm not ready" had been my litany.

At one time, while on my knees and bawling like a baby, I simply surrendered and totally, unconditionally, turned over to this Higher Power all my vain struggling. Immediately, I felt a very warm, extremely loving Presence in the diagnosed area of my body. It felt like a Light moving within me and out through the soles of my feet. The movement was swift, precise and clear. This Force felt like the most natural and peaceful thing in the world.

As soon as I felt this, I stopped crying, got up immediately and went about my ordinary chores. I felt no need to pray about it anymore or even think about what happened. It was a done deal and I just knew I was healed. That was 12 years ago and the subsequent medical evidence supports that I am healed.

 *Love notes to mySelf*

12

ON GUILT

As women, we've been unconsciously programmed to feel guilty if we're not nice enough or not pretty enough, not anything enough. It takes a lot of courage to silence what "common sense" dictates. Who wrote those unspoken "laws" anyway?

Historically, a patriarchal society. It was done not out of anger but simply out of fear. Women were perceived as a threatening but necessary presence instead of as friends and companions.

Love notes to mySelf

13

ON FORGIVENESS

I realize I cannot truly love if I don't forget and let go all past hurts. We all want to be loved. But we will not and cannot receive love, even from the best-meaning people, while keeping some past injury or hurt remembered and thus unforgiven blocks us.

This is when tying up all loose ends counts so much. Years ago, I pretended I had only four weeks to live. It was surprising for me to face what I had been procrastinating about for the hundredth time. One of the things I did was write a letter to my ex in-laws. I spoke from my heart, asked for their forgiveness and for their understanding, and said I didn't know any better then because I was so full of myself. Without editing and completely trusting my Inner Guidance, I mailed it. The results were and still are very positive, beautiful and loving. How could they not be?

In a different context, you forgive Bob and Alice for how you perceived they didn't appreciate you. So you create the vacuum and consequently the time and space for Harry's love to come into your life.

Love notes to mySelf

14

ON "TAKING THE PLUNGE"

Ads in magazines say things like "Just do it!" But it requires so much unwavering, almost blind faith and courage to take that bold leap.

Using another analogy, it's like a trapeze artist. You have to let go of that one bar to be able to connect to the next.

It's the space between the bars that's the scariest part but also the most necessary. The time seems horrifyingly magnified when you're not holding onto anything at all.

To me, this is the only kind of freedom. It is freedom to let go of any old attachments and wearisome pinings for what-might-have-beens. It is letting go equally of the usual manipulative speculations for what should be.

Essentially, it is a freedom <u>from fear</u> and a leap into the light.

Love notes to mySelf

15
ON LISTENING

Listening to body rhythms, plain intuition, and my Self is an extremely nurturing and simple thing to do.

In short, I "did nothing" yesterday except purposely slow down. Most important, by doing this exercise, I did not feel guilty about it.

Instead, I trusted my instinct that said ... "this is just an exercise I need to do constantly, which is necessary in order to be plugged-in to the Divine Current."

In "doing nothing," I found my energy level rise to newer heights and spread down into deeper levels. This made being kind and loving yesterday an effortless accomplishment.

Love notes to mySelf
....

16
ON BEING AFRAID

As often as I allow it, I'm not ashamed to admit to myself and to others that I am afraid. My shyness, reluctance and even defensiveness are caused by my fears.

After this admission, I then get a nice, warm, strangely new feeling that it really doesn't matter what "they" think about me being unconventionally true to my feelings.

In doing so, the Real me, the true Self gets unblocked.

As a result, I am sure I make some people uncomfortable. Being aware of my fears and admitting them serves as an unconscious reminder to others of their own hidden, but not buried, fears. I learn about my own fears from others as well.

Fear—whether it is anxiety, doubt or trying too hard— happens when I forget to connect to my Inner Higher Self.

Love notes to mySelf

17
ON TALKING UNNECESSARILY

I watch myself when I say superfluous words because it is an indication of where my mind is at that time. My ego is into self-importance and its inevitable companion, cluttered and pretentious thinking.

When I greet someone with the perfunctory "How-are-you?" and other social inquiries, I want to mean it. If I don't really mean what I say, I'm wasting my Life Force by using superfluous words, which I so routinely and wantonly did before.

Words are energy forces. They can cut us down and paralyze us or lift us up to our noblest level. We chatter needlessly, thus robbing ourselves of true communication with others. When it is our turn in the conversation, we embellish ourselves, instead of keeping to the story or to the point, as if really keeping it simple would lessen our value.

Love notes to mySelf

18
On career pressure

At work, I saw a person and circumstance that reminded me of a past incident that had made me uncomfortable. This caused me stress. Surprisingly, I realized it was my own nagging fear of self-worth that I was angrily reacting to.

I'd push certain people far away or shut my mind off whenever they would talk. I saw I was reacting to them as Reena, the ignored child, who as a youngster was neither fully encouraged nor discouraged by her fighting parents.

So, I doubted my own worth. I found that I even doubted my gut feelings. The inevitable accompanying blocks would follow. On the one hand, I wanted success. Yet on the other hand, I was unaccustomed to anything that reminded me that I could really have it.

Consequently, I labeled this as "pressure."

Love notes to mySelf

19
ON BEING KIND

Coming from the usual dysfunctional family, I had a very hard time allowing the concept of love to move out of my head and down to my heart.

Like most women with this background, I thought love meant being the perfect wife or perfect girlfriend, etc. Thus, it was a constant efforting.

I awoke one day and realized this couldn't be "love." I knew I needed some tools, so I went through a lot of studies, spiritual classes, prayer and basically "getting down on my knees." By using these tools, I have hacked my way out of that underbrush, through the trees and out of the bushes.

In this small clearing, my intuition just tells me to pause.

The little glimmer of light I see says, "Just be kind." Be kind to the tired and seemingly inept sales clerk, to the people in their cars honking behind me, and to myself by buying that flower to brighten up my room. In its simplest form, you make the time to be kind.

Doing so brings that big word "love" down to a very practical place within me. It nurtures my soul.

Thus enriched, I can then go out and spread this lightness of being to my daughter, her friends, my friends, co-workers and all the different people I encounter in my simple everyday world.

to mySelf be true

Love notes to mySelf

20
ON JOURNALING

I cannot say enough about how critical and essential journaling is for women. We have so very many feelings that we try to sort out in our heads while juggling our busy lives.

When feelings are not sorted out, it shows in the tenseness around the eyes, the areas between the cheekbones and jaws. No amount of make-up, facials or expensive outfits can camouflage that.

Writing down our feelings—either when we're feeling victimized, or while rushing maddeningly by on the fast track—slows us down. It's a check-and-balance system.

Against all logic of linear time, journaling amazingly enables us to do what has to be done with less effort and better results. It unblocks us.

Does it sound too good and simplistic to be true?

The simple solutions are where our ego is the most resistant.

Think about that before you complain again about not having time for journaling or for yourself.

to mySelf be true

Love notes to mySelf

21
ON SEX

More sex will not create more intimacy. Again, it's the other way around.

The lingerie, candles, frequency, etc., are just about outer forms, not inner content. The latter, and the connecting, is what we as women are really looking for.

As long as I kept focusing on the outer forms and proportionately neglected my inner personal and spiritual growth, nothing satisfied me.

Stop and ask yourself, "What really is the big difference here between what is good for me and what is right for me?"

When confronted that way, I always call to mind my grandmother's equally wise answer: "What is good is not always necessarily right. But what is right is always good."

Turn the TV off. Set aside the magazines that distract you from yourself. Quiet your self, so you can <u>hear</u> your feelings.

It is when you listen, remember your worth and are intimate with your real inner Self that the energy, whether sensual or otherwise, just oozes out from you.

Being happy by knowing yourself more makes you sexy and attractive. It leads the way to intimacy on all levels.

to mySelf be true

Love notes to mySelf

22
On praying

This is one of my many necessary tools for anchoring. Without it, I scatter my Force and Energy needlessly, think unnecessary thoughts, do redundant and peripheral "busy" things.

When do I know a thought and action are unnecessary?

When it strays from my goals of being more kind and loving to myself first and then to others or when I don't feel the peacefulness.

It is important to discern when religiosity becomes an unconscious cop-out or screen. The principles and accompanying rituals should instead be seen as merely tools to be used with good, old-fashioned, down-to-earth practice, practice, practice!

For example, there are many forms from countless books and other sources on how to pray. I always get results when I am in my most simple and heartfelt state, with prayers like: "God, please help me. I can't see and I don't understand. Please just help me trust only You."

Love notes to mySelf

23

ON STARTING A NEW DAY

In our sleep state, when our brain or ego is stilled, we are very connected to the Power.

Upon awakening, around 6 a.m. or earlier, and for most of the day, I do not turn the TV or the radio on. Remember, I said most, not all, of the day. When I stop all the clamoring of those machines, I get to hear myself.

Something within "tells" me whether I should pick up an inspirational book, sit quietly to wait and listen for guidance, or to journal now or later in the day. Sometimes anxiety creeps in and the cacophony of noise in my head anticipates the busy day awaiting me. That is when I call to mind Jacob in the Book of Genesis and his willfulness in obtaining God's blessing. In the story he wrestled with the angel until dawn. Like Jacob, I say it repeatedly: "I will not let Thee go, until thou hast blessed me."

Once I receive His blessing and accompanying peace, my mind clears. Then I hear "… this is good for me, that is the right step to take, or this is to be avoided for now." I am surprised to hear myself!

It feels energizing that the Self I'm hearing is not the fearful, insecure personality anymore, and that being validated by similar outside voices is not necessary.

It feels right and very peaceful.

Then I take my daughter to school and start my day.

Love notes to mySelf

24
ON DOING
WHAT HAS TO BE DONE ANYWAY

With a changed attitude, there's a certain feeling of accomplishment after doing the most mundane, seemingly repetitious chores.

While doing simple chores, our thoughts are never about "the work." They're about the past ("Gosh! I've done this before") or about the future ("What if I get too old" or "I can't afford it").

When our thoughts are in the present moment while doing <u>anything</u>, the shift in attitude becomes the exciting part. It's almost unbelievable that such an ordinary, commonplace little shift would make getting the work done seem almost like a rite of passage.

The simple remembering of letting go <u>all</u> thoughts of the past and future and just <u>being</u> in the present makes each ordinary event become symbolic, a little victory, just between God, the lamppost and me.

Love notes to mySelf

25
ON "PLAYING"
WHILE DOING EVERYDAY CHORES

It doesn't have to be a big, pre-planned block of time. It can be a purposeful funny cookie when scraping the last of the cookie batter, a '70s or '80s cassette while driving to meet a deadline or anything that will remind me <u>again</u> that things on my to-do list are <u>not</u> things on a do-or-die list.

I catch myself this way and ask: What am I trying to prove? To whom and for what? Is it going to make me kinder and gentler to my family and friends because I did everything on my, by now, must-do list?

A phrase I heard a lot growing up which we hardly hear as often now is "take it easy." Perhaps when everything is going crazy around us, we ought to listen to the wisdom of those three words.

Again, take it easy. That's part of playing.

Love notes to mySelf

26

ON CANDLES AND ROMANCE

I plead guilty to having candles around me but always waiting for special occasions to use them again.   The dark colored string atop the melted wax makes a pretty picture, which easily gives me the illusion that I gave in to the romance of candlelight. Never quite totally, always holding back a little. This is because of the subliminal message from movies and TV that says the romance of candlelight must and can only be enjoyed with another person.

Testing you and myself, I ask, "Exactly how long ago was the last time that candle was lit?"

The romance of a lit candle adds sparkle to the air around me. Even though it's just writing my thank-you notes, thumbing through a magazine or reading an uplifting book.

We strategically place these lovely candles, here or there for someone else—the lover, the girlfriend, the dinner guest, etc., and never ever really just for us, for me, female, period.

I want to celebrate my learning and my mistakes, to celebrate how far I've come, to celebrate the discovery that I am becoming more healed and whole everyday.

Thus, from this position of strength, I share this contentment, joy and light with others.

Love notes to mySelf

27
ON SIMPLICITY

More often, under the guise of intellectualism or even religion, it's easier to be complicated than to be simple.

I know that when I don't feel peaceful about any matter, I've complicated the thing. When it's deciding what to do next, instead of listening to my inner Self first, my brain goes every which way. I feel harried and unsure.

It's not easy to be simple. I have a tremendous amount of respect and admiration for those few people who actually are.

They are my teachers.

Love notes to mySelf

28
ON RESENTMENTS

It is impossible to truly feel love, whether giving or receiving, when there is resentment. The other person, be it husband, boyfriend, girlfriend, sister, brother or child, could be giving you more but you're not seeing it because of your resentment.

Yet on the other hand, even when you think you're giving love to this same person, you're depriving yourself of the fuller joy and deeper reward of giving. This is because your resentment is blocking you.

Unconditional love becomes just a meaningless phrase without forgiveness.

In my life, I am amazed how often I have to work on forgiving. That's because I'm realizing how many layers of small resentments have built up through the years. I was trying to be "nice" instead of being honest to my self, my true inner Self. I was trying to be "a peacemaker" for the sake of the family, which of course produces everything but that, as long as I was feeling resentful.

Resentment, much like forgiveness, is an energy that can be sensed and felt before it is seen and heard.

to mySelf be true

Love notes to mySelf
·······························

29
ON ASKING FOR HELP

When I was in my twenties, my 90-year-old grandmother gave me a piece of advice. I thought it was ridiculously exaggerated.

My grandmother was someone who never went beyond the third grade, yet succeeded in earning a lot of money and buying an enormous amount of real estate. She never got sick, had a sharp mind even in her last years, was loved for her humility and died peacefully in her sleep.

What amazes me is that I just recently read in a magazine that very same advice she gave me many years ago.

It is this: "Ask God for help a thousand times every single day." For example, what to do, what to say, where to go, what do You think of this, and so forth.

"A thousand!" I would feel like a nagger.

Since I had tried everything else to no avail, I figured I had better just follow her advice and ask for His help every step of the way. What did He want done or said through me?

After some practice, I stopped struggling and thinking too much. I started to experience what "being in the Flow" meant. Everything became easier and lighter. It continues to be so.

What my grandmother was trying to tell me was to seek God's Kingdom. "Only and always," she would add, and all things follow.

to mySelf be true

Love notes to mySelf

30
ON BEING LOVED

Such a basic universal need! It has become a
desperate cry in the '90s. Everyone is too "busy." Everything
has become as common as a byte.

That is why I find it so important to slow down. Slowing
down reminds me that the love I seek outside of me must first
start within and with me.

I nurture and gift myself.

An example of gifting myself would be forgiving myself
first before thinking of forgiving the other person. A less
profound example would be keeping the perfect piece of toast
for myself.

It could even mean what society terms as a "selfish
woman." I call that being true to my Higher Self. This Higher
Self deserves to speak, be heard and never settle for less.

When I nurture and gift myself this way, I find a very
childlike, natural lovingness swelling up within me. Because
It feels childlike, I allow It to express in very simple words,
a sincere look or small gesture.

The biggest surprise is that the perceived meanest-
person-on-earth in front of me that moment is always only
too willing to be good, to do good, to love me back in his
own little or big way.

In spite of our repeated forgetting, love is indeed our
natural state.

46

to mySelf be true

Love notes to mySelf

31
ON STRONG WOMEN

They are the backbone of any society. They are also history's and today's unsung heroes. When all the women in a society are morally and emotionally strong, they lift all men and children to that state. In addition, the successful man always had a strong woman sometime in his background, who planted the seeds of his success. She could be a sister, grandmother, friend, wife, lover or mother.

A strong woman

doesn't feel the need to prove anything at all.

moves only from a position of inner strength.

is not afraid or ashamed to cry, to admit when she's right, and does not fall all over herself when she's wrong.

knows she gets stronger as she extends her light to others in the world.

has no guilt about being born a woman thus has no excuses for settling for what the world has been giving her.

respects her femininity and never uses her body unlovingly.

I salute women like Rosa Parks, Barbra Streisand, my grandmother, Golda Meir and Mother Teresa. In the same breath, I also praise those countless women in ordinary lives overcoming extraordinary circumstances.

32
ON PLAYING

A prerequisite to playing, of course, is to notice when you're taking yourself too seriously. This is when things are "not happening" and you're exhausted from trying too hard.

One need not even get into some "formal" gear to play.

I remember when I was little, while seated in the car on a long trip, I'd look at the clouds, make and see funny images. I still do similar things like that on airplanes.

Playing is a childlike attitude. Children instinctively know when they have to move along and when they can play in between the gaps in that moving-along process.

Playing should not be a big deal or a major production. We were not created to be dead serious.

Love notes to mySelf

33

ON DE-MESMERIZING ROMANCE

On the one hand, we're addicted to romance, "the one", we think. We believe such a relationship will fix or complete us.

On the other hand, we also want to think we're these strong, independent warriors marching off into the 21st century.

Both beliefs are so ego based. They will never make us happy. The romantic relationship is so strong it pulls us away from God. We've made our little idols and given them the power to make us happy or sad.

It is only through a very committed spiritual journey that we learn to de-mystify relationships and have the strength to pull away from this seduction.

Really letting go and letting God is the scariest thing in the world. I got so sick and tired of being so sick and tired, I just had to do it.

Once I let go and took the plunge, not surprisingly, I immediately received the natural, simple and deep love that at an earlier time, I had been struggling and grabbing for.

to mySelf be true

Love notes to mySelf

34
ON THE "PARALYSIS OF ANALYSIS"

This is another way we get and almost stay stuck. It seems the right job or relationship is just not coming about. "What else must I do or not do?" we ask.

My guru taught me a very basic, sure-fire, timeless remedy.

She called it the "ING" mode. The what mode?
Sure, instead of thinking the word love, you are lovING.
Instead of just the word forgiveness, you are forgivING.

It's about action that begets other action in your life.
It's also another way of saying "Don't think too much!"

Love notes to mySelf

35
ON NOT JUDGING

I used to think I wasn't judgmental of people anymore. As is the case with any denial, there was a lack of peace within me.

Of course, a partial admission only meant justifying and defending my silent mental judgement.

How, in my world, can the Universe give me a break when I'm not giving others a break?

Love notes to mySelf

36
ON LONELINESS

It is hard to digest—let alone believe when I read or hear—that loneliness comes when we're separated from God.

"But I'm a good and successful wife, or mother or career woman!" we protest amid our restlessness and isolation.

Yet we have received much, so we have to give much, too.

Whenever I feel this, I immediately do my "brownie points." Like a true Girl Scout, I look for 10 people I can do a good deed for daily.

Most of the time, it is a seemingly unappreciated kindness in the form of a simple smile, words of encouragement, or an unexpected thank-you note to the postal carrier.

You know deep in your heart that this works. I always have guaranteed happy results within 24 hours.

So, I remember again, that loneliness is just another form of energy. Used negatively, we know what it can do and how we hurt ourselves more. Used positively as a reason to reach out to help others, it moves our focus from a "just me" perspective to one of a common bond, a unity with others.

The "feel-good" feeling is permanent.

to mySelf be true

Love notes to mySelf

37
On
"PEELING THE LAYERS OF THE ONION"

Some of us have worn so many masks we have forgotten what we were trying to cover.

Ultimately, it's always a fear: of not being loved, approved of, or good enough.

I had to eat a lot of humble pie for a long time to be open and willing to ask for genuine humility. It takes a lot of that virtue to be able to face yourself, especially to peel away one more layer of fear in its various disguises.

What are some of its countless forms? How do we mask our feelings of unworthiness? By working too much. By obsessing about romance and our looks. By trying too hard.

Love notes to mySelf

38
ON GETTING SICK

When I have even a slight headache, I know I am a house divided.

It wasn't because I had to do this and that. It was because I let myself get run over by what I perceived were my duties in life, as opposed to focusing on my duties to myself first.

That means setting boundaries.

So I backtrack in my head to within one or two days. The culprit is usually the incident when I didn't respect my feelings and intuition enough to say yes or no to external demands.

The same goes for colds, although they have a longer gestation period. I was wrongly spreading myself too thinly for others and for their approval.

The constant efforting wears out our nerves. The resulting suppressed, everyday irritation is what runs us down. That is why we get sick.

Love notes to mySelf

39
ON WRITING THANK-YOU NOTES

A fax or e-mail just doesn't do it.

There is a part of our heart that we want to share when we do something special. Choosing our own way of saying something (whether on stationery or out loud) forces us to face one more hesitation of being exposed or unmasked. Writing thank-you notes is a very simple and genuine way to reach out to someone.

If I just look at how happy they would be because of my gesture, I forget my brain's constant, limiting kind of thinking. You know, the kind that says I can't-do-this or don't-do-that.

The graciousness and magnanimity of thank-you notes are as much for me as they are for the other person. That is what elegance and style are all about.

Love notes to mySelf

40

ON LETTING GO AND LETTING GOD

This is a much-used phrase nowadays.

There comes a time, though, when it becomes used almost automatically and most of all, unfeelingly.

You recognize this stage when things aren't going the way you thought they would.

You're stuck. Again.

There is a seemingly fine line that needs to be crossed and calls for discernment. At this time, I ask myself: "When do I let go and when do I move my feet?"

As always, when I've moved through and away from the various shades and shadows of my ego, I find myself wanting to be as childlike as possible in asking for guidance.

Letting go and letting God is much like allowing ourselves to free fall with no net.

In free fall, there comes a time when God catches you.

Then you'll know just what, when and how something has to be done.

You'll know it's right because of its accompanying peace.

Love notes to mySelf

41
ON FEMALE EXPECTATIONS
OF OUR SIGNIFICANT OTHER

We heap all our unconscious expectations onto
one male in whatever stage in life we happen to be. This
is whether he is a father, husband, lover or boyfriend.
Women have been conditioned throughout history, to view
themselves as unfinished and incomplete unless in a
relationship. This is not the Truth about us.

We think a relationship will complete us and we bring
that belief with us when we get into one. "If I could just
find completeness with and through him, then I'd be happy,"
we murmur. "He's got it all," we continue. Naturally we
get disappointed.

This inevitably brings us back to having to look within
ourselves for the Answer. "There is a Higher, Complete Self
within me," I say.

The numerous fringe benefits from going within
prevent me from putting all of my expectations on one
equally unprepared and unwary male.

So I find my joy in discussing history and politics with
Tom, sharing my emotional awakenings with Uncle Dick and
having fun with Harry. In short, I apportion to several males
in my world, the princely qualities that I impossibly expected
from just one person.

Love notes to mySelf

42
ON ATTRACTIVENESS

Being truly attractive is an internal, spiritual thing, more than what all the latest female-targeted magazines tell us about what we should do to be "cool, sexy, etc."

After the initial physical intrigue, what attracts us to or repels us from another person is usually an unexplainable energy that is sensed. This energy has a lot to do with how they value themselves. They know who they are.

Haven't you noticed that the really attractive, almost charismatic people are those who are happy with themselves?

They're not constantly efforting. That's why they're so attractive.

Love notes to mySelf

43
ON CHANGE

In our wanting to be in control of our fate, even our declarations of wanting change in ourselves are so conditional.

"Okay, this is as far as I go. I'll 'rest' here first," we say.

What we're really saying is "I'll stay here in this comfort zone."

I've learned that this causes a big traffic jam in my life.

The Universe is always current and I wasn't.

Love notes to mySelf

44

ON FORGIVING MY PARENTS

Not only did they "not know any better." They just didn't have the kind of tools and support for higher awareness and understanding that we have in the '90s.

I thought I had worked on forgiving my parents from day one many years ago. Such naiveté and even arrogance to assume I was done with my forgiveness work.

The fact that I kept repeating certain patterns in my life, even though it was getting easier and easier to get out of those negative cycles, convinced me I still hadn't forgiven them as much as I thought I had.

In short, I forgave only in my head. It hadn't and couldn't reach the very core of my heart precisely because I didn't acknowledge <u>all</u> of my own feelings in relation to them. It was about trusting and then feeling cheated, deprived and hurt.

Hitting bottom is never as bad or as horrible as we imagine.

It's surprisingly very relieving.

Love notes to mySelf

45
ON ENTHUSIASM

I read that "enthusiasm is a spiritual commitment." Whenever I sense I am on the fringes of boredom, I know that some time not too long ago, maybe within the past few days, I allowed myself to believe in the seductions of the world such as my career or my money.

I had missed a turn and gotten disconnected from my Source.

The simple prayer of "Please, please, get me out of Your Way" releases me from these paralyzing mind games and then I'm able to do what must be done.

The work is done easily, happily, in perfect timing, and beautifully, too.

Love notes to mySelf

46
ON SENSUALITY

I enjoy being sensual.

It is acknowledging my femaleness without guilt and without using my body unlovingly.

One of the ways we use our bodies unlovingly is when we use our sensuality and its trappings to attract a man or men. You have to honestly ask yourself, "What is the real reason why I feel I have to strut my stuff?"

Again, attraction is an effortless thing, much like a magnet. Using the same analogy, just keep working on yourself. The personal properties of a magnet (in this case, you) are strength, calmness and clarity.

The sensuality and subsequent attractiveness becomes natural, a given.

Love notes to mySelf

47

ON LIVING
ONLY AROUND THE PERIPHERY OF LIFE

When you only <u>think</u> you're happy, you're living in your world peripherally. You even have to rush to say it to your friends and relatives as if doing so convinces them and yourself that you are indeed what you claim.

When you have to convince someone else of your claim, then you know something is not right.

Happiness is not a thinking thing. It's a knowing thing. The knowing permeates every cell in your body so that it not only radiates in your eyes and smile but also in your words and actions. You feel it.

I used to work in the gift industry for many years. My fast track then involved product designing, sourcing, manufacturing, shipping, exporting/importing, warehousing, wholesaling and retailing. After a serious illness, I decided to re-evaluate my life. I did a lot of volunteer work during that time and wondered if that was well, er ... life. Later on I journaled that, "if I'm going to be so busy loving, then I won't have time to make money."

That was a big joke, of course. I still associated making money or having a special relationship as the accompanying price tag for happiness.

Making money, in contrast to attracting opportunities which cause me to make money, much like other outer forms, seemed so real. If it was indeed my reality, then why was I always craving for something else? It's like there was an invisible, gaping hole I needed to fill and yet I never made a dent in it.

Everything became a crutch—the power, the relationships and the success. I knew I had to lay down those crutches if I wanted to be at the center of Life, my life.

When I laid down those crutches, it became very clear to me to follow my heart, in this case to paint and to write.

When you follow that intuition and follow your heart, you're alive. You are energy personified. You are right on target because you are centered.

Love notes to mySelf

48

ON BOREDOM AND BEING BORING

Boredom is such an ego thing! I used to paint the very same thing in an identical manner using the same colors and mood over and over again. I couldn't understand where my creativity went.

There was no spirit in my work because there was no genuine love there. I was doing it for the money and the praises. I had also started to take myself very seriously, again.

One of the best ways to monitor yourself is to do a monthly or quarterly "Life Values Chart." Julia Cameron introduced a similar exercise to me in her book *The Artist's Way*. Get a piece of paper and date it. On a scale from 1 to 10, evaluate yourself on these six areas: spirituality, love/adventure, work, play, exercise and social/friends.

At one time or another, I found myself overly involved in one or two areas. When I'm sweating the small stuff, I know I'm way too serious. Keeping tabs on your "Life Values Chart" makes you aware of what caused your imbalance.

I post that little chart conspicuously in my dressing room, on my mirror, in my bathroom and daily planner. I also update it on a regular basis. This is a very easy and effective way I catch myself before I get bored with myself or become too boring for company.

I am so busy working on me, I don't have time to judge others, gossip or complain. New unexplainable, revitalizing energy emerges. I'm excited and enthusiastic.

I am having a love affair with Life!

Love notes to mySelf

49
ON GRATITUDE

This is a major cornerstone.

In a profound manner, it is everything and it brings you everything.

I never could understand those bumper stickers I'd see, proclaiming that "Perfect Love Is" or " God is all."

I needed a more practical explanation to bring it to my everyday, ordinary earth life. Surprisingly, remembering to be grateful constantly, for all the seemingly little things (my old car, my new carpet, my old released thoughts, all my new positive thoughts, etc.) was actually practicing love.

How simple! I didn't have to read volumes of self-help or spiritual books to feel loving. Most importantly, I experienced the feeling of being very loved by this kind, ever-present Force.

Love notes to mySelf

50
ON CRYING

It is crucial. That is if you want to get on with life, move forward and be in the Flow, of course.

As women, we've been programmed to be patient until we become the patient at some doctor's clinic ourselves.

That kind of stuffing feelings in—for the sake of "peace" in the family or because it's considered bitchy in the office and we're supposed to be "nice" —is why it's necessary to cry.

To release pent-up emotions, yes. More to the point, to acknowledge the gut feelings that our minds automatically discarded. The message I got when growing up was the importance of just being good. Nobody told me: "be happy."

In crying, we clear the body's system for its even, natural and normal flow.

Love notes to mySelf

51
ON RELIGION

I am wary of too much attachment to religion and its rituals. They can easily be used to manipulate and act as smokescreens to our natural Light. One can also run away and hide behind religion, but never for long. I know I did.

However, I felt a constant, indescribable longing of my soul. I wanted to give and receive love more but didn't know just how to do it.

Later on I saw that religion and its beautiful rituals were just mere tools to help me get through my darkness and find my own Inner Teacher.

Love notes to mySelf

52
ON TITHING

To tithe means giving 10 percent of your gross income to the places, institutions or persons from which you receive spiritual food. It acknowledges that God is our source. Tithing on a regular basis is giving back to the Universal Soil. It is very much like the farmer who <u>must</u> replant after he has harvested and taken from the soil.

I used to think that given my financial resources, I couldn't afford to tithe. Just remember that farmer analogy and you'll tithe quicker than you can say, "Hmmm ... wait a minute."

In the beginning, tithing forces us to be creative in making do with the balance. Then what look like little miracles start happening.

Tithing is my connection to the Universal Soil. I know on a very human level that I have the right and deserve to receive from my Source when I tithe conscientiously. Tithing taps our feeling level too, which is a prerequisite for the real knowing. That is when things begin to happen.

Everything including relationships and events start jelling. You can't tithe and be bitchy and mean. How could we be? It is a loving giving back to Our Father.

53

ON PLAYING SMALL

When I'm trying to prove something to others, cleverly masked as proving something to myself, I get disconnected from the Divine Current.

I knock myself off center this way. Sometimes I get knocked off first by somebody else's remark or action.

Playing big, however, requires a lot of simplicity and humility.

As women, we have played small all these years. We were taught this role from our mothers and their mothers before them. We have more gifts, talents and insights than we allow ourselves to accept. It is in this historic cusp wherein we have not only found our voices by playing big, but also we are finding each other and our unbelievable strength as well.

It is unbelievable strength.

That is why I cannot afford to play small anymore.

Love notes to mySelf

54
ON RAISING
MY 15-YEAR-OLD DAUGHTER

She is my mirror. If I perceive her as cold and uncaring, I know I should not get upset at the image I see.

I work on myself. I go "within" first before going "without". There is an automatic guarantee of change in the image ... in this case, my teenager.

It's hard to think of teen-agers in the same breath as miracles. It is the same breath.

I want her to be the better version of me at that age. Any which way you look at it, you can't go wrong with that.

Love notes to mySelf
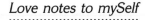

55

ON TAPPING YOUR FEELING LEVEL

This has been written and talked about. We pride ourselves with our intellectual gymnastics. We take action only on the thinking level, consequently, we have become afraid to feel. We don't let even our deepest feelings about ourselves surface, let alone show them.

Mixed with the ego, thinking and feeling can get messy.

But if the feeling is really coming from deep within our hearts and our souls, we will be protected from what we think is just our vulnerability.

I realize most people are fearful. My attempts to sincerely express my caring feelings will never leave me empty.

Do whatever it takes to tap your feeling level. Music always does the trick for me. In moments when I feel off center, I allow myself to let go with the music. If it's a classical piece, I'm either the conductor or the ballet dancer. Alone in my room, of course, I let it weave its magical spell on me. A more modern piece has me gyrating accordingly.

I love to laugh at myself during these times. I bring that joy with me when I leave my room and go forth into the day.

Love notes to mySelf

56
ON WRITING THIS BOOK

At one time, I had some doubts as to why anyone would want to read about such simple musings.

The answer is because I've reached a place in my life where I can try to help others who are floundering like I was and are not even aware they are floundering.

There was just an anxiety that happiness must be out there somewhere. It's not out there of course. It is within.

Love notes to mySelf

57
ON SPOILING YOURSELF

I happened to talk to an acquaintance, a flight attendant, who was taking her allotted yearly vacation.

Aside from the prerequisite R and R, I suggested that she spoil herself. At first she was a little surprised and hesitant; then a big "Aha!" and a "Yes!" lit up her face.

This is not about being spoiled rotten and consequently off-balanced. This is about reminding ourselves that we most certainly deserve to spoil ourselves, under the right circumstances and without any guilt whatsoever.

Once again, to just do it.

It almost equals a leap of faith. In truth, it is just that ... a leap of faith in and for yourself.

Love notes to mySelf

58
ON FEAR AND DEFENSES WITH PEOPLE WHO LOVE YOU

Over and over again, like a wave that keeps hitting shore, the message came to me that I could only honestly and authentically love back as long as I knew myself. This was necessary so I could truly forgive myself.

Not knowing myself made it such an effort to "love back," in the ways I thought were love. It tired and confused me and was always very conditional.

Knowing yourself takes a lot of work. More than anything, it requires a lot of courage to keep peeling away those layers of the onion.

When you get to the core—the perceived scariest place—you will have to ask for the most faith that you can muster. Yet you will never, ever be alone.

As a matter of fact, you'll realize you were never alone to begin with.

It is from this knowing that you are not alone, that loving becomes natural.

Love notes to mySelf

84

to mySelf be true

59

ON BEING IN KINDERGARTEN

Zen calls this the beginner's mind.

I get my lessons, learn to stretch, leave my comfort zones and play in this class. Sometimes I find myself at the back of the class because I've been unruly or thought I was so special.

That's when I realize that I need to be there and to remember that I have to be a team player, an Indian and that I can't be the chief all the time.

Being in this class is fun. Since I have no grandiose expectations when I'm in my kindergarten mind, I get to accomplish things easily. I am constantly aware that I don't know it all and the joy is in the learning.

Love notes to mySelf

60

ON CONTINUING PERSONAL GROWTH

We pride ourselves in thinking we have an open mind. Our quiet but ignored intolerance or mild annoyance of others' beliefs and practices say the opposite. Yet we continue to gather together in search of something.

I believe in doing what is necessary to get there (classes, books, church or support groups) and finding that something that drove me to take that route in the first place. I also believe you need to stop all of that for a while.

You let it sink in and then you rest from all that spiritual information.

Do something else ... your soul will stir you to the right activity. Much like everything else in nature, we observe the ebb and the flow, the within, then the without.

We remember to enjoy this precious little pocket of space in our lives.

Love notes to mySelf

61

ON ROMANCE AND MALE FRIENDS

We use that phrase so conveniently. With a flippant attitude, those words ("let's just be friends") just tumble out of our mouths.

We think we're cool.

Actually we're still confused on where the lines are drawn.

Why? Our ego wants to think of every man, or most men, as attracted to us, as subconsciously a conquest.

Our denied need for this kind of validation blurs our thinking.

A girlfriend of mine was going through the first courtship stages and getting very upset that he didn't do something or whatever.

I asked her, "If Andrew were Reena, would you be <u>that</u> upset with me?"

"No," she countered "because you're my friend."

"Need I say more?"

We laugh at those cartoons that show dollar signs in a character's eyes. Romance is the same thing, except it is hearts and flowers in our eyes.

As long as he was seen only that way, she could never be a friend to him whether they continued on or broke up. "Let's just be friends" would just be another play on words, cheapened by misuse instead of being elevated to its best and most glorious state of loving.

Love notes to mySelf

62

ON BEING COMFORTABLE WITH ONESELF

As much as I desired the word authenticity to apply to me, somehow it kept eluding me.

This was because I was on a 40-m.p.h. road travelling only 35 m.p.h. all the time. Of course it's not surprising to see other people give you the look as they go by.

In short, if I decided to be on that particular road, I realized I needed to "pay the price" or speed up.

Being authentic takes a lot of facing our denials and what we are pretending not to see about ourselves.

Our well-meaning friends and loved ones tell us, but we brush it off with a "Yes, but…" or "They don't really, <u>really</u> know." Mere acquaintances, even strangers, repeat the message. We chuckle and say it's pure coincidence, accidental. "And besides," we say to ourselves, "I'm too busy being busy."

Oh yeah?

Then the Universe comes with its big wake-up call, usually painful by this time because you kept on pretending until you couldn't pretend anymore.

You get on your knees and you stay there. You stay in that space, stripped of all defenses of pride and fear in its many countless forms.

It's like any withdrawal and, yes, not easy at all.

But were you comfortable, content and at ease in that lifestyle before the withdrawal?

Love notes to mySelf

63
ON "SEARCHING"

There's a line in the book, *A Course in Miracles,* that says, "Searching means you have not accepted."

I thought I knew that very, very well intellectually. As always, things take a long time to filter down to my heart. I had covered it with so much stuff! I was protecting that child from being hurt again.

So in later years, I thought … "If I just cling to my mind, my brains, then the part of me that was hurt will be protected by my thinking."

It doesn't work that way, thus the restlessness.

Owning my feelings, then not judging them, whether I was being very ugly, unChristian or not "nice," was the start.

Take 15-minute daily walks alone.

Journal. Nurture yourself. Clean out all your old stuff, including papers and clothes not worn in the last two years. Help somebody, anybody!

When you know you're on the right path, you'll feel the peace. It won't be a search anymore and you won't feel so desperate.

Love notes to mySelf

64

ON LINGERING TOO LONG
IN THE LOST-AND-FOUND DEPARTMENT

Except for the last couple of years, historically and culturally, women thought they had to be "found" before they got a life, thus the creation of the prince-will-save-me fairy tale and its even more damaging lost-lady-in-distress syndrome.

In spite of our degrees and accomplishments, this fantasy continues to keep us from soaring even higher. Uncorrected, it becomes our Achilles Heel. We either feel some guilt when we do spread our wings and start to take off or we feel a secret jealousy at some woman who did dare to fly.

I was in the lost-and-found department for a long time. The roller coaster ride of emotions made me sick to my stomach, until I finally and figuratively puked.

That was the best part about leaving that department.

Love notes to mySelf

65
ON GOLDEN MOMENTS

It's much like Maria Von Trapp's song about her favorite things in *The Sound of Music*.

In my everyday life, it only takes a few seconds to acknowledge and be grateful for:

my woolies on a cold November night;

the warmth of the flannel sheets;

the time between turning the lights off and settling in;

the fact that instead of worrying about the TV news, I'm practicing Omnipresence; and

falling gently and deeply into sleep.

Love notes to mySelf

66
ON BEING A FEMINIST

What exactly does that mean?

Men say the word or ask the question "Are you a feminist?" almost distastefully. We are either noisily defending or quietly consenting with our silence.

We work so hard to correct this myopic concept of us by competing aggressively.

If that is the only reason, our "why", then no wonder we're battle-weary.

We don't have to fight it out.

Being a feminist means just being true to our own nature. If we can continue to remember that and purify our thoughts about being feminine, we will be making our own rules. Men have no choice really.

Love notes to mySelf

67
ON GROWING PAINS

Symptoms of not yet facing the truth about ourselves are when we are either profusely apologetic or indignantly defensive.

Neither of the two is necessary.

What to do?

The first step is awareness.

The second is asking for help either directly from above or indirectly on the earth level.

The third is to get moving with consistency.

Like physical exercise, consistency is vital.

Happy growing!

Love notes to mySelf
....

68

ON SHARING MY "BIG" SECRET

I journaled this a long time ago. In mining for nuggets to include in this book, I decided to include this entry.

"As a young child, I was ashamed of and repeatedly shamed by the public's late '50s perception of a divorce and its ugliness. I was almost apologetic for existing, now that I think of it. I felt no worth in being around but since I was already around, I figured that if I tried to be lovable, I would be loved. So I tried to always be nice and perfect, or more attractive or more the center of attention so I would be lovable."

I cry for this hurt child. Nobody told her she had any worth at all until much, much later. She thought snatching, competing and efforting was a way of life.

Though my parents' divorce caused me sorrow, I was made strong by this experience and became the person I am today. A little bit of a late bloomer here, but blooming nevertheless.

Looking back at this entry for the last time today, I can now just say, "Hmmm! Wow! Interesting! Let's get going and move on!"

Love notes to mySelf

69
ON FOLLOWING YOUR HEART

Following your heart doesn't necessarily mean following a passion, whether with a certain someone or with your creativity. I've learned it also means following this almost basic gut feeling which we've covered with our to-do and must-do scenarios.

A friend of mine picked me up at the airport at 10 p.m. on Sunday. After a very busy weekend and an equally long flight, I thought I just needed to be home ASAP.

We "played it by ear," so to speak, and spent the next 45 minutes over coffee, just talking and really connecting. I left for home, totally energized and happier.

That's why spontaneity is always so right in feeling and in results. The flowing does indeed take care of me when otherwise I think something should be followed only according to my mind.

Please trust those feelings more.

Life should not be such a hassle.

Love notes to mySelf

70
On commitment

Any commitment, whether social, emotional, financial or spiritual, is proportionately equivalent to a person's awareness and respect for commitment to herself or himself.

I used to think I scored "10s" on all levels except emotionally. My desire to score perfectly in the other departments only made me more aware I was making up for where I scored the least.

By this time, I realized that any way I went, turned, denied or hid, I still had to face me. Together with a sincere desire to really grow, the me I was masking was turning out to be my true Self, naturally good in every way.

Half commitments are fakes. It's like prostituting life and myself. Settling for so very, very much less.

I've met a few people, who, in spite of their great fears are committed in all the areas of their world. Maybe they're scoring "8s" in all areas, for now.

These are the ones with the real passion for life. They are "all there" and Life blesses them magnanimously.

to mySelf be true

Love notes to mySelf

71
ON LONELINESS AND PACING YOURSELF

Others can feel our loneliness. We ignore our own loneliness, of course, and cover it with shopping marathons, eating or starving binges, overdrinking, or being obsessed with a perfect form or body.

To get off this fast track, one has to take the first exit and pull over.

You assess what you're doing and why you need to be on the fast track anyway.

Taking that first exit before getting back on the freeway means having to be alone for a while. At first, it looks and feels like a very, very long time. Just keep trusting your instinct.

It was when you didn't that you got lonely.

Love notes to mySelf

72
ON MEMORIES
OF PAST RELATIONSHIPS

The deadly word here is memories. It is a seductive word dripping with nostalgic illusions. It blurs our vision and blocks us from savoring all the gifts of the present.

Mixed memories—you know, remembering the good mixed with the "bad"—are worse. They are like boundaries that you move about at your convenience. You think you have that control. This is not so.

You know this from your up and down emotions.

At one time, I was trapped in this kind of quicksand. The only way out was to completely forgive him and myself. I forgave all the "bad" memories, seeing only the good and the beautiful lessons I learned to become a better person. I forced myself to see only the good in him that attracted me in the first place.

During all of this, I asked continuously and persistently for God's help. I turned over to Him my anger, cynicism, despair, disgust and pain.

There are no grays with mixed remembering. It's either black or white. Choosing one over the other removes the boundaries.

It frees you up.

Love notes to mySelf

73
ON CONGRATULATING YOURSELF

This must be done often, on an everyday, every moment basis. It breeds contentment with yourself instead of constantly seeing all your faults.

I congratulate myself for even the smallest, seemingly insignificant, things: for buying the perfect teacup, every single time I drink my morning tea and for the Neutrogena bath products I love to use everyday.

On a less mundane line, I congratulate myself again and again for my resiliency and capacity to accept change and for my desire to share simple insights.

I am all of these and more, so very, very much more. Isn't that the best reason for congratulations?

Love notes to mySelf
....

74
ON THE CORRECT USE OF TIME

I was visiting a friend in jail who introduced me to an inmate. He was taking classes on history and ancient civilizations while, ironically "doing time." There was a spiritedness that was emerging from within him. The source of his activities was the determination that he would use the time to overcome exactly that, time, by learning.

It's never about being busy—it's always about learning.

That shift in our mind enables us to move about our day in a here-and-now mode. Being fully in that mode erases past regrets and future worries.

Simplicity itself!

It takes a lot of awareness to be simple.

Love notes to mySelf

75
ON INNER STRENGTH

Inner strength begets balance. Like purification, there are quite a number of steps to take before reaching this higher ground. This is the only journey worth taking.

Most misfortunes force us to look within ourselves for the Power to go on and make it through. It usually starts with that kind of wake-up call. Unfortunately, we rely on this alarm clock and then turn on the snooze button and then wonder why our life is the way it is.

I believe the only reason I didn't go over the edge when I was much younger is because I innocently believed there was some unnamable Something that took care of me in spite of my riotous living.

Later on, I learned I could call on this Something, even if all I said half to myself was "I'm afraid. Please help me!"

As I fine-tuned this process, I learned some pretty basic principles to keep me in that vibration where my calls for help were answered more and more.

One of the most valuable of these is learning to make time for yourself. You don't have to go to Tibet. For example, just let the machine take all your calls until you're ready. You already have all the answers. You are just blocked temporarily. Don't ever forget to ask your Inner Guide for answers.

Many times my frantic efforts to storm Heaven's gates with "I don't understand this" or "I can't see" are indeed silenced when I ask for His peace first. Later on, doors start to open. It's guaranteed.

Only then do I walk through those doors from a position of strength.

Love notes to mySelf

76
ON CHALLENGES

When God is your Anchor, there are no challenges.

If anything, the only real challenge is changing your old negative, fearful way of thinking, so ingrained and so unreliably real to you.

Why "take on" the world and tire yourself needlessly? Why feel guilty about relaxing?

That means trusting your Anchor.

We all know that it is when we've relaxed our "must" kind of thinking, that the best and perfect ideas come tumbling forth. We know it is right because we move and act on it. Best of all, we're very happy while doing it.

So, what was the big deal about that "challenge"?

Love notes to mySelf

77
ON PSYCHICS

We're all psychic. Some of us are more tuned in to others' wavelengths and frequencies. The psychics we visit are much like antennae.

Your fate changes or stays on course to the exact degree of your core belief. Psychics pick that up when you're in your confused state. Not that going to a psychic is in itself bad, as long as instead of being addicted or dependent on it and on them, you realize that they are just another tool to be used to get you out of being stuck.

Later, hopefully much sooner than later, you will have no need for psychic readings as you listen more and more to your own Inner Teacher.

Love notes to mySelf

78

ON SUPPORTING OTHER WOMEN

I guess most of us are unaware of how ambivalent our feelings are about successful women and women who are still struggling.

The supreme irony is how we can give 110 percent support to a man in a "romantic" relationship, yet have some reluctance giving support to a woman precisely because it is not a romantic relationship.

Considering the many female writers and women who have reached a certain level of power, I'm surprised how conditionally supportive we still are of strong women in our everyday lives.

In supporting them, we're actually giving that kind of support to ourselves.

Love notes to mySelf

79
ON SUFFERING

Viewed correctly, the best thing about suffering is that it makes us humble.

It is from this position that healing takes place and will continue. It is comforting to know that suffering is not our natural state. Wholeness is.

That's another great reason to open that bottle of wine and celebrate again!

Love notes to mySelf
....

80
ON ADOLESCENT ANGST

As a young teenager, I really didn't know I was lonely. I just felt it, but didn't recognize it.

I <u>bless</u> all those lonely moments. They are very beautiful because they were the means to bring me to this level.

In my desire for happiness, those lonely moments propelled me to take plodding steps, the first of a thousand steps from adolescence to womanhood.

Though my steps were usually quite filled with drama, I knew I'd get somewhere safe as long as I held on to my Anchor, and sure enough I did.

It is a safe, loving place. I'm very happy there and here. God's world and my world are now fused as one.

Love notes to mySelf

81
ON SIMPLIFYING

I know I don't need all those pairs of shoes and all my closet paraphernalia. I have a yearly garage sale and am amazed at the stuff I still need to unload and stop hoarding.

We marvel at the idea and wonderful results of simplifying our lives, yet we constantly take on new things. It's akin to being afraid of being alone with ourselves.

Every single step we take is daring ourselves: Am I going to do this conditionally again?

Love notes to mySelf

82

ON DISAGREEING WITH THIS BOOK

You are free to disregard some or all of the shared thoughts and realizations in this book.

Do whatever it takes to bring you peace. But for Heaven's sake, take the step and complete it with action and practice. There are so many ways to get there and so many of your loved ones and friends waiting for more of your kindness.

<u>Shine even more!</u>

to mySelf be true

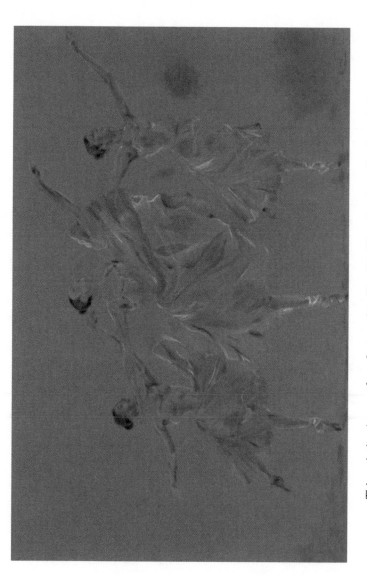

Freedom from Fear

This painting is one of my first works. The title "Freedom from Fear" is a beloved reminder to me everyday that I can indeed be free from all of my fears, if I continue to be honest and loving to mySelf first.

How to reach us

If you would like information about our newsletter,
retreats or seminars, please call us or write to us at:

Bridges Publishing
2183 Buckingham Rd., Suite 152
Richardson, TX 75081
(972) 889-8668

Order Form

to mySelf be true is a loving and thoughtful gift for family and friends.

To order additional copies, please fill out the information below and mail a copy of this form with a check or money order— made payable to <u>Bridges Communication, Inc.</u>—to:

Bridges Publishing
2183 Buckingham Rd., Suite 152
Richardson, TX 75081

Name   _____

Address   _____

City   _____State_____Zip_____

Phone   _____

to mySelf be true

Book(s) Cost: $14.95 x _____(Quantity) = $_____

Shipping & Handling: $3.75 for first book. + _____
                       See chart below for
                       additional copies.

Texas residents please add 8.25% sales tax   + _____

Total amount of Check or Money Order $_____
(made payable to Bridges Communication, Inc.)

Shipping & Handling Rates		
Under	$15.00	$3.75
$15.01 -	$30.00	$5.75
$30.01 -	$45.00	$6.75
$45.01 -	$60.00	$7.75
$60.01 -	$75.00	$8.75
$75.01 -	$100.00	$9.75
$100.01 -	$150.00	$11.75
$150.01 -	$200.00	$13.75
Over	$200.00	$15.75